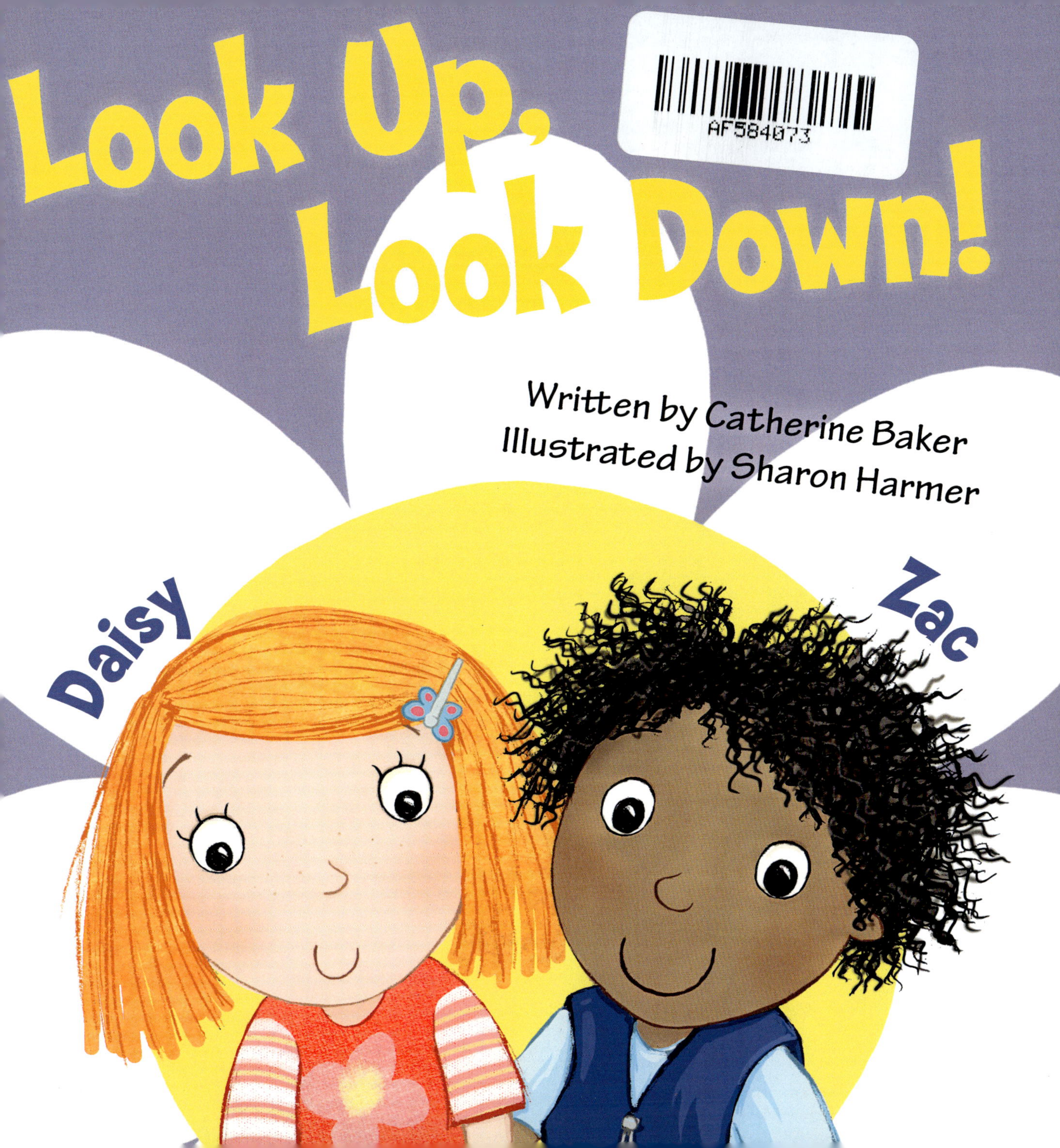
Look Up,
Look Down!
Written by Catherine Baker
Illustrated by Sharon Harmer
Daisy
Zac

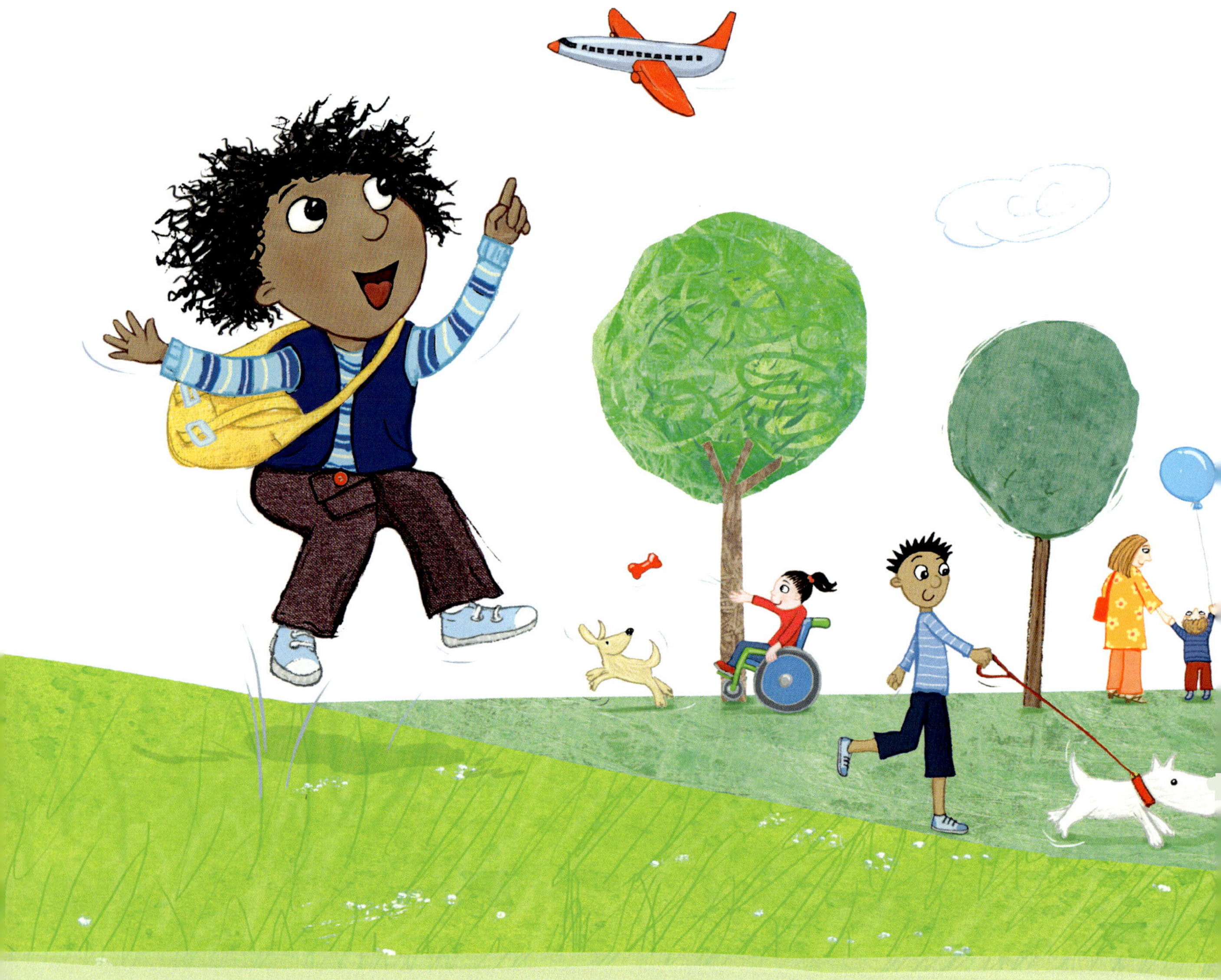

I can see a jet.

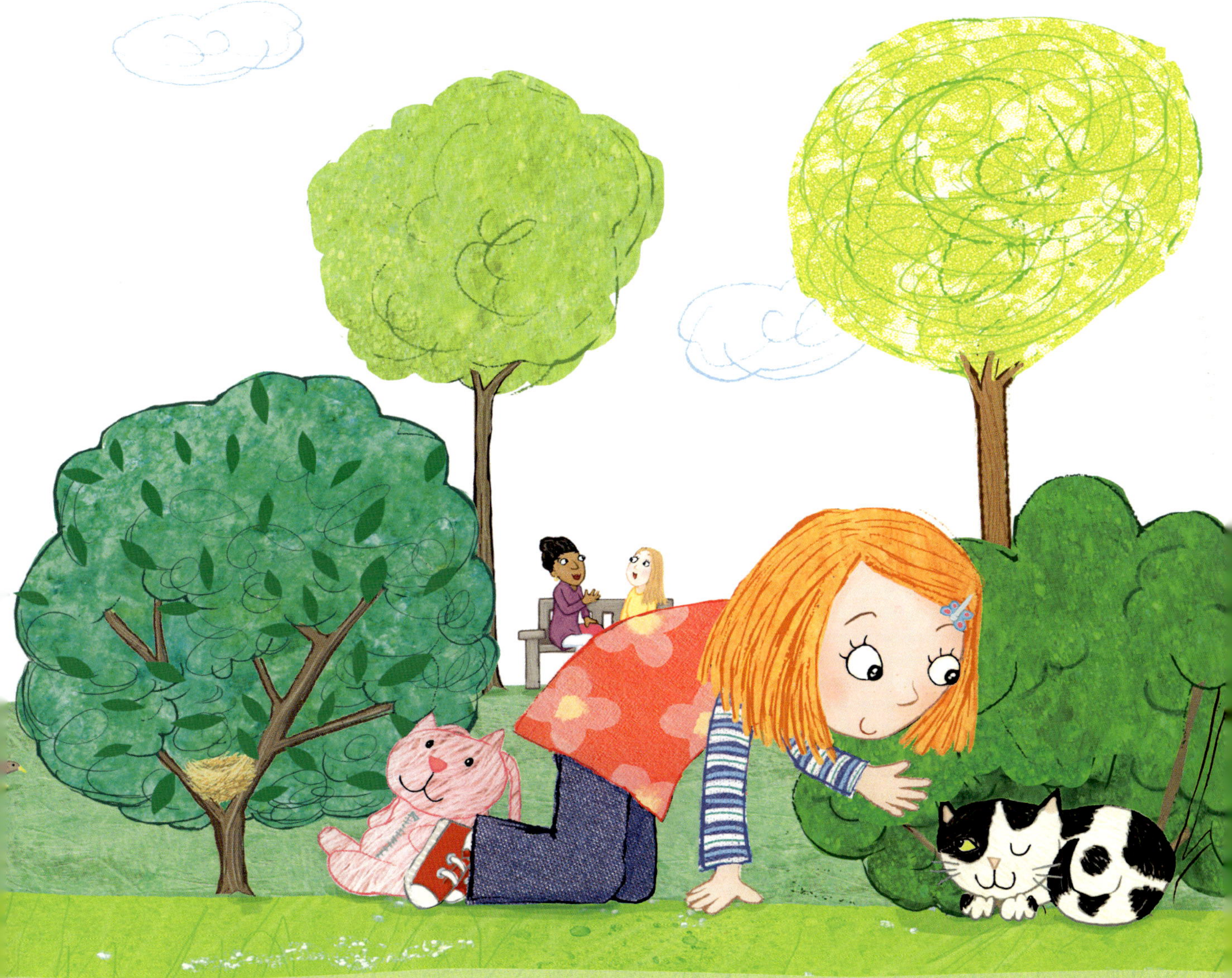

I can see a cat.

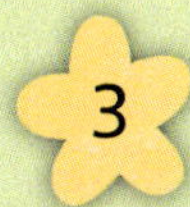

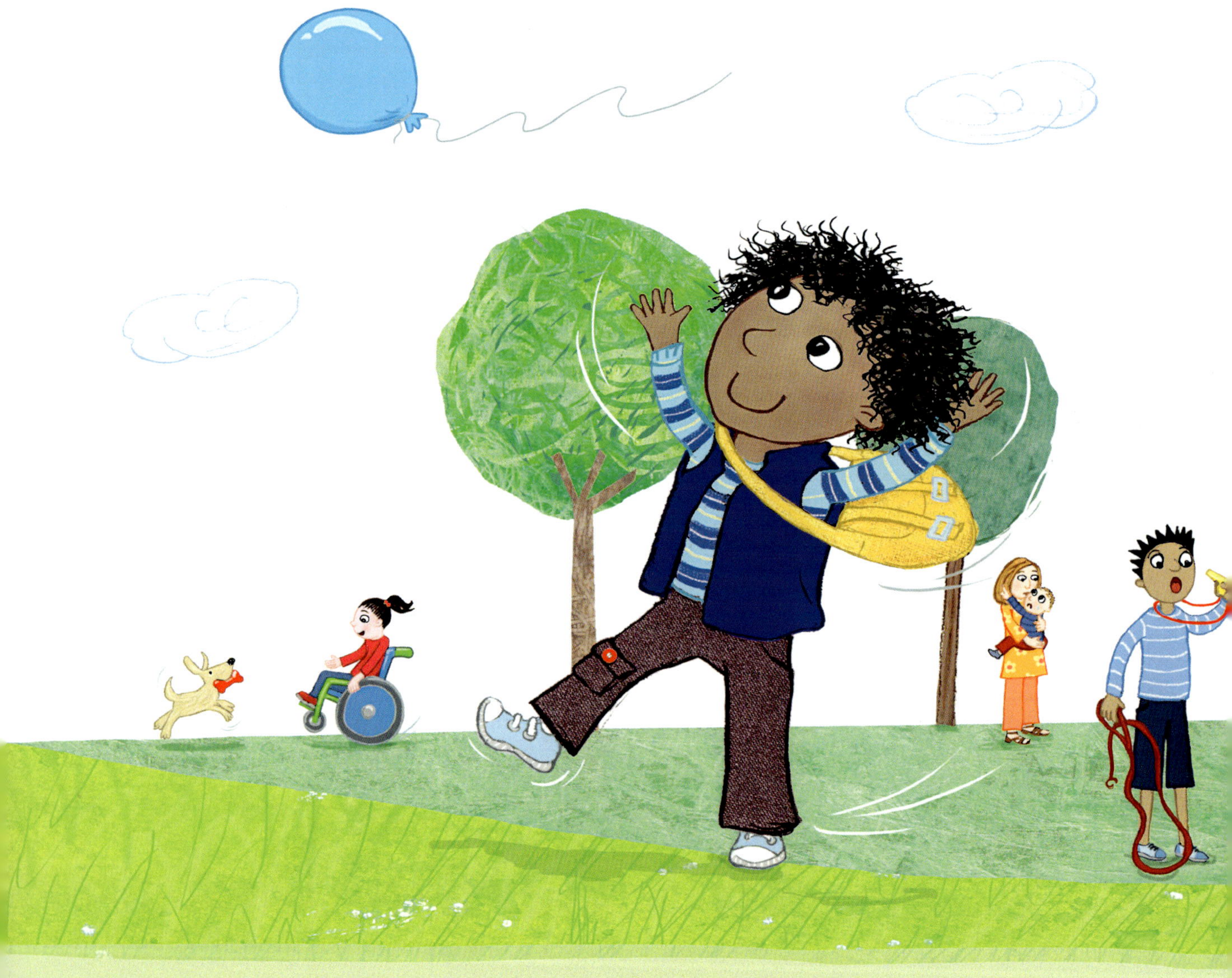

I can see a balloon.

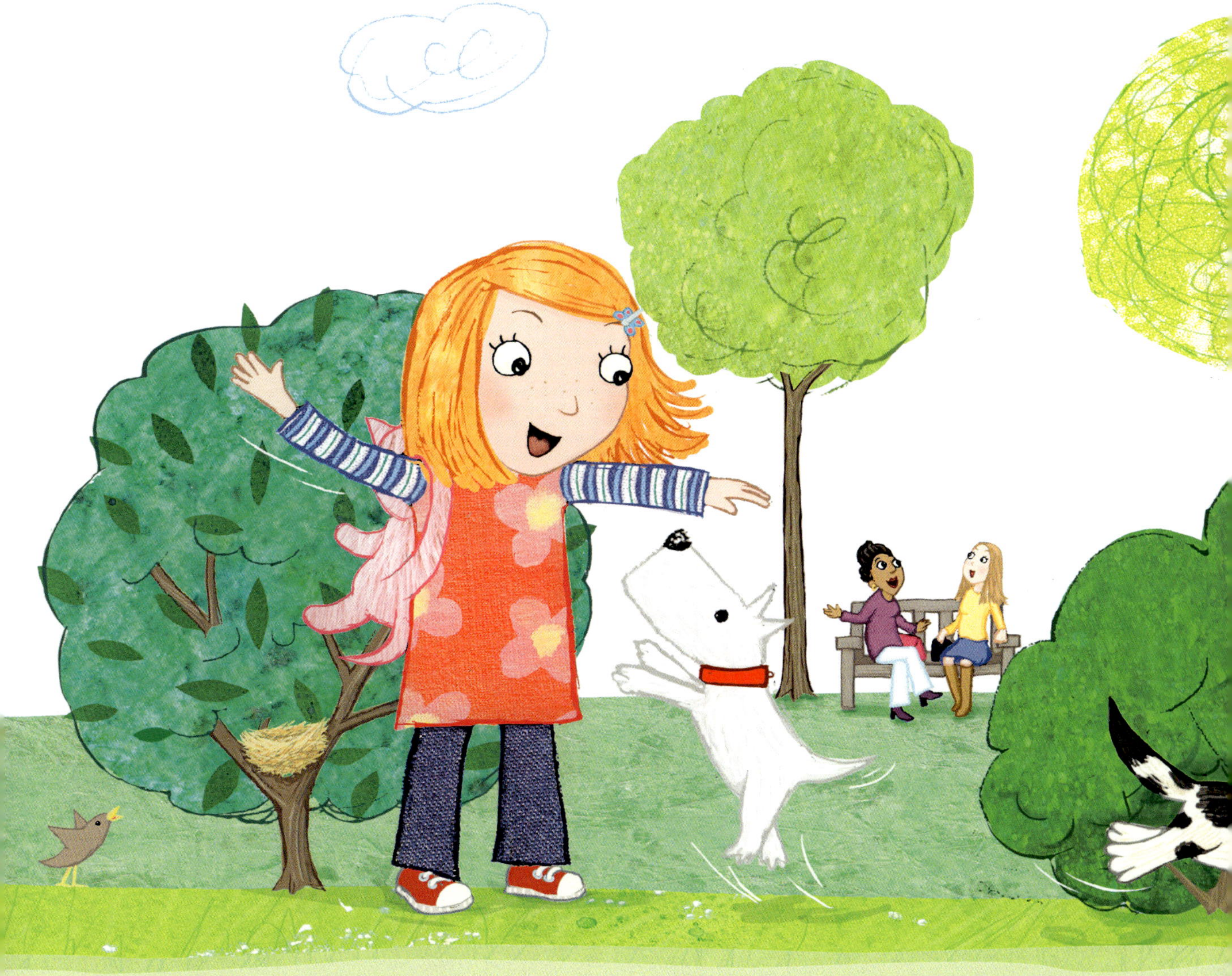

I can see a dog.

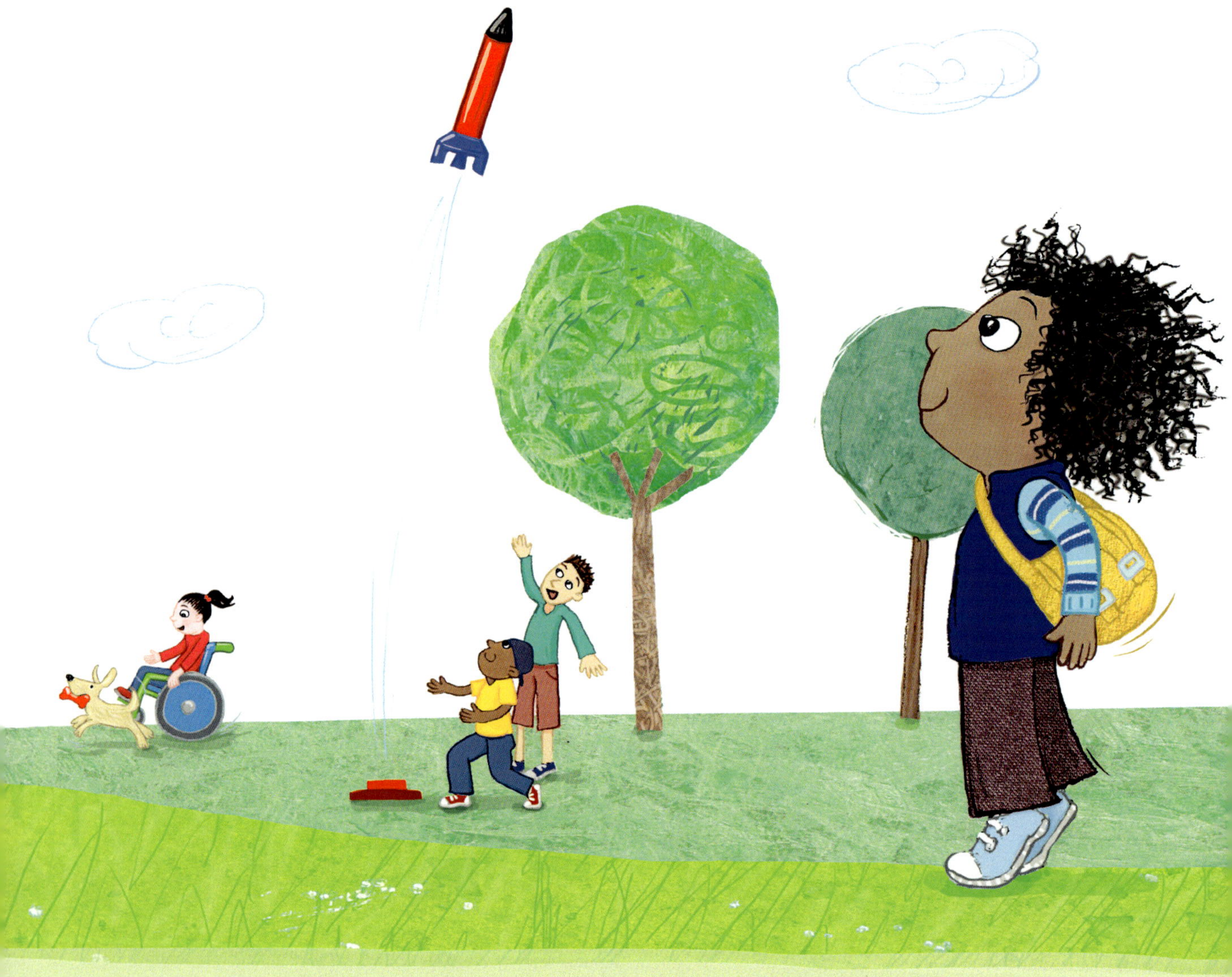

I can see a rocket.

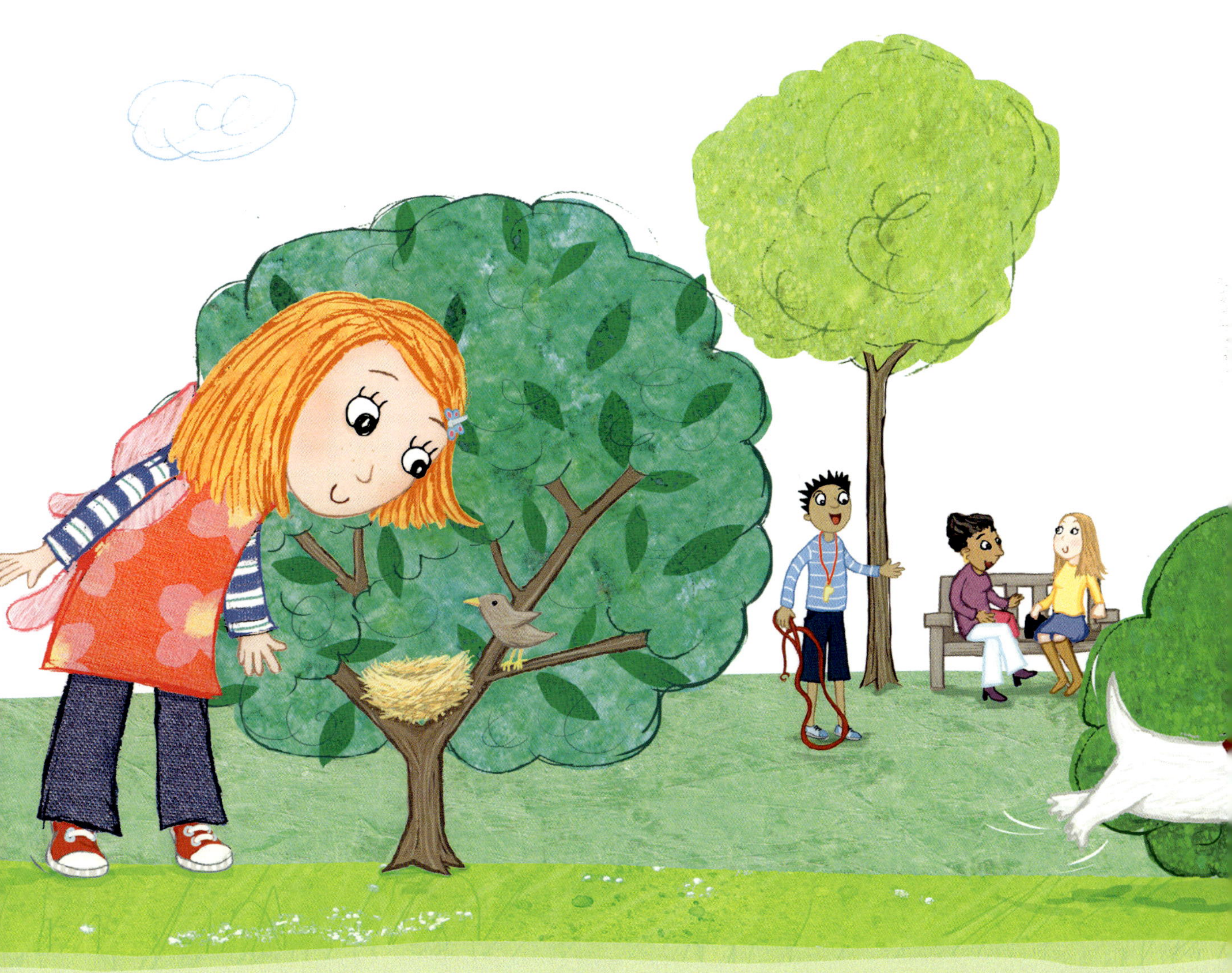

I can see a nest.

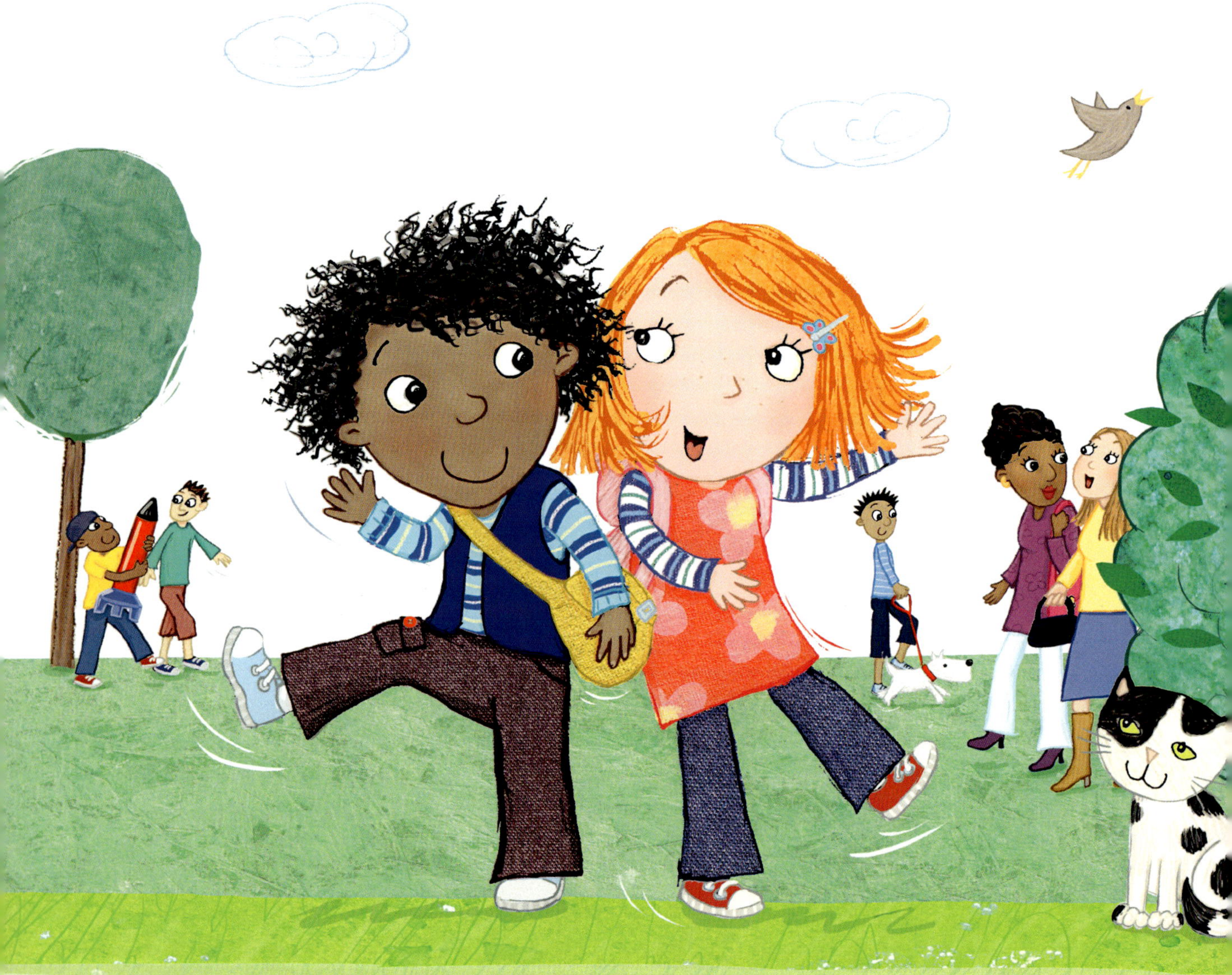

I **did** **not** see you!

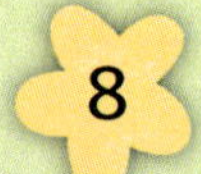